# The Seven C's of History

by
*Stacia McKeever*
and
*Dan Lietha*

## Answers in GENESIS

PO Box 6330 • Florence, KY 41042 • USA
www.AnwersInGenesis.org

First printing: January 2003

ISBN: 1-893345-10-6

Printed in the United States of America

*Table of Contents*

Most children (as well as their parents) look on the Bible as a book about Jesus—and about salvation—one that contains lots of interesting stories and teaching about how we should behave as Christians.

All of the above is true, but the Bible is much more than this—it is a *history book* that reveals the major events of history that are foundational to the message of salvation and morality.

Sadly, generations of children have been brought up to see the Bible as just a book of teaching that is not connected to physical reality, but by and large deals with only abstract things like feelings and behavior.

This limited viewpoint explains why many children don't know how to explain dinosaurs, fossils, death and suffering, and many other topics that relate to the real world children live in.

This curriculum, entitled *The Seven C's of History,* is the first in a series of teaching resources that will help children (and adults) see the Bible as *The History Book of the Universe.* This history, which outlines the major events of the past (and the future), will enable students to develop a Christian worldview by putting on 'Biblical glasses' (representing these historical events) so that they can properly interpret the facts of the present (e.g. dinosaurs and fossils).

continued next page

The more students are able to develop this Christian worldview and wear Biblical glasses, the more they will be able to defend the Christian faith, to know why they believe what they do as Christians, and to be able to challenge the skeptics of the age and effectively present the Gospel, which is based in a history that can be trusted.

It is my prayer that this curriculum, based on the storyline of the *Answers in Genesis* Creation Museum, will equip coming generations to reconnect the Bible to the real world and thus be able to challenge the secular worldview that so dominates our Western culture today.

Ken Ham
President, *Answers in Genesis*

**Stacia McKeever** graduated *summa cum laude* in biology and psychology from Clearwater Christian College in 1997. She has worked full-time for *Answers in Genesis* (USA) since then, and co-authors the 'Answers for Kids' section in each *Creation* magazine. Stacia has written or co-written a number of articles for *Creation* magazine and the AiG Web site, and periodically leads workshops centered around the '7 C's of History' for children at AiG seminars. She lives with her husband, Seth, in the Greater Cincinnati Area.

**Dan Lietha** has been drawing since he was a child. He graduated in 1987 from the Joe Kubert School of Cartoon and Graphic Art, and has been a full-time professional cartoonist since 1991. Since joining the *Answers in Genesis* staff in 1997, he has illustrated several books (including *A is for Adam, When Dragons' Hearts Were Good* and *The Great Dinosaur Mystery Solved!*), created comic strips for the AiG newsletter and Web site, and produced countless illustrations which the AiG speakers use to effectively communicate the message that God's Word can be trusted from the beginning. He and his wife Marcia currently reside in the Greater Cincinnati Area.

Dear Teacher,

The following series of lessons (recommended for ages 7-11) will take you and your students on a journey through history from the very beginning of Creation until the very end of this present world, highlighting the major events that have affected (and will affect) the entire universe. We call these events *The 7 C's of History*.

These lessons will help you and your children to understand that the Bible is *The History Book of the Universe* and will enable you to uphold your faith in today's increasingly secular society. Many times, Biblical accounts are taught as mere 'stories'—nice tales that may have a moral message but lack any connection to the real world. This series of lessons explains how to reconnect the Bible to the real world of geology, astronomy, biology, etc., thus enabling everyone to be ready to 'make a defense to everyone who asks you to give an account for the hope that is in you' (1 Peter 3:15). It is important to teach children that the Bible tells the truth when it touches on these areas (geology, biology, etc.). Otherwise, they may wonder, 'Why should we trust the Bible when it speaks about salvation if we can't trust the Bible when it speaks about these other things?' (John 3:12).

*Creation* reveals that God created in six normal-length days around 6,000 years ago.

*Corruption* shows that Adam's disobedience brought death, sickness and sorrow to the world, thus leading to the need for a Redeemer.

The *Catastrophe* was the global Flood of Noah's day by which God judged the wickedness of man.

 The *Confusion* at Babel came when God confused the language of Noah's descendants, causing them to spread out into various tribes and nations all over the Earth.

 *Christ* (the Creator God who stepped into history to become a man) came to redeem the world from sin by dying on the *Cross* and paying the death penalty for those who receive Him.

 We look forward to the *Consummation* of all things in the future, when the Curse will be removed and God prepares the new heavens and the new Earth for His children.

Some teachers may wish to just read the weekly handouts with their students, while others may desire more in-depth teaching, which the teacher's notes for each 'C' will provide. (You may wish to break up each lesson into shorter lessons, depending on the length of your class time.) Our Web site <www.AnswersInGenesis.org> contains vast amounts of information that will supplement each of the C's.

We trust this curriculum will be a blessing and encouragement to you and those in your class.

Sincerely,
Stacia McKeever and Dan Lietha

# *C*reation
In Six Days ...
c. 4000 BC

**Text:** Genesis 1:1-2:3
**Memory verse:** Genesis 1:1

Some people believe the universe is billions of years old. It is often pictured as coming from the result of a giant explosion. These people believe that everything around us (and we ourselves!) came from a series of accidents happening gradually over millions of years. Others believe that God used *evolution* to 'create' over millions of years. Still others believe that God created progressively over millions of years.

But these views do not agree with the Biblical record. The Bible, God's Word to us, records the *true* history of the universe. It gives a completely different account of how everything came to be and what has happened since then. The Bible reveals that God didn't use evolution to create and that the Earth isn't millions of years old.

Use the third page of this week's handout, 'The first Six Days are history!' to introduce to your students the fact that God created all things in six normal-length days (not over long periods of time).

Have students open their Bibles to Genesis 1, and open their handout to the first page, *Creation*.

### ◆ **Read Genesis 1:1-5.**

**Day 1:** God created light. This light was separate from the sun, which wasn't created until Day 4.

Ask:    How can we have 'day and night' without the sun?

We know today that all it takes to have a day-and-night cycle is a rotating Earth and light coming from one direction. The Bible tells us clearly that God created *light* on the first day, as well as the Earth. Thus we can deduce that the Earth was already rotating in space relative to this created light. This sequence of events would later have been very significant to pagans, who tended to worship the sun as the source of all life. God seems to be making it pointedly clear that the sun is secondary to His Creatorhood as the source of everything. He doesn't 'need' the sun in order to create life (in contrast to theistic evolutionary beliefs), and He even warns against worshiping it (Deuteronomy 4:19).

### ◆ **Read Genesis 1:6-8.**

**Day 2:** God separated the waters above the expanse from the waters below. He formed the atmosphere needed to support the life that would soon be created.

Note: If you are familiar with the 'vapor canopy' model, please note that many creation scientists are now either abandoning the water vapor canopy model or no longer seeing any need for such a concept. Regardless, it is a model and should therefore not be taught dogmatically. (For more information, see chapter 12 of *The Updated and Expanded Answers Book* or the essay 'Where did the water come from?' <www.AnswersInGenesis.org/flood>.)

## ◆ Read Genesis 1:9-13.

**Day 3:** Dry land appeared and God created various plant kinds, which would be food for the animals (including dinosaurs) and humans created on Days 5 and 6. The creation of plants on Day 3—before the sun and animals—is contrary to the beliefs of evolutionists and other 'long-agers' who teach that plants arose long *after* the sun came into existence.

> **Note:** The Bible makes a clear distinction between the status of plants and animals. Plants are not *alive* in the Biblical sense. People and animals are described in Genesis as having, or being, *nephesh* (Hebrew)—see Genesis 1:20–21, 24, where *nephesh chayyah* is translated 'living creatures,' and Genesis 2:7, where Adam became a 'living soul' (*nephesh chayyah*). *Nephesh* conveys the basic idea of a 'breathing creature.' It is also used widely in the Old Testament, in combination with other words, to convey ideas of emotions, feelings, etc. Perhaps *nephesh* refers to life with a certain level of consciousness. Plants do not have such *nephesh*, and so Adam's eating a carrot did not involve 'death' in the Biblical sense.

## ◆ Read Genesis 1:14-19.

**Day 4:** Sun, moon and stars were created for lights, signs, seasons, days and years. The Moon's revolution around the Earth is the basis for our month, and the Earth's revolution around the Sun is the basis for our year. The tilt of Earth's axis determines seasons. But the only basis for the seven-day week is found in Genesis 1 (and reiterated in Exodus 20:11).

Some people ask, 'If the universe is only a few thousand years old, then how can we see light from stars that are over one billion light-years away?'

One possible model that helps to explain the answer to this 'puzzle' has been proposed by Dr Russell Humphreys. Einstein's theory of general relativity tells us that time is not the same everywhere in this universe, but instead can run at very different rates, depending on the strength of the surrounding gravitational field. With certain initial conditions at the Creation, a literal day or two could have passed on the Earth while from 'the light's point of view,' it had millions or even billions of years to get here. So the entire universe was created in six ordinary-length Earth-rotation days, 6,000 years ago (by Earth clocks). Such things are possible as a consequence of general relativity, which is simply a description of the universe as accurate as we are able to currently determine. For more details, see chapter 5 of *The Updated and Expanded Answers Book*, found on the Web at <www.AnswersInGenesis.org/starlight>.

## ◆ Read Genesis 1:20-23.

**Day 5:** God created flying creatures, including flying reptiles (such as pterodactyls) and water creatures, including plesiosaurs, whales, etc. This is contrary to the supposed order of development found in the fossil record, allegedly representing millions of years of Earth history, which has land animals existing *before* birds and whales.

## ◆ Read Genesis 1:24-26.

**Day 6:** God created land animals (including dinosaurs) and the very first people. This means that dinosaurs and humans existed together—not millions of years apart.

## ◆ Read Genesis 2:7-25.

This section of Scripture provides a more detailed look at the events of the Sixth Day of Creation.

After God formed the first man from the dust of the ground (not from an ape-like creature!), He assigned Adam the task of naming the various 'kinds' of livestock, birds of the air, and beasts of the field that He brought before Adam. Obviously, Adam was created with the ability to speak and reason—it didn't take millions of years for humans to develop these abilities, as some people believe.

Note: Bible-believing scientists are actively involved in researching the boundaries of the original **created** kinds of animals. The Biblical **kind** is not necessarily the same as what we call a species today. A working definition of a created kind is: if two animals or two plants can mate and produce a truly fertilized egg, then they must belong to (i.e. have descended from) the same original created kind. For example, if the animals are from different **genera** within a **family,** it suggests that the whole family might have come from one created kind. If the animals are from genera in different families within the same order, it suggests that the whole order may have derived from the original created kind.

On the other hand, if two species will not hybridize (mate together and produce a fertilized egg), it does not necessarily prove that they are not originally from the same kind. We know of human couples who cannot have children, but this does not mean they are separate species!

Following are some examples of hybrids that show that the created kind is often at a higher level than the species, or even the genus, named by taxonomists:

1.  Liger: offspring of a cross between a male African lion (*Panthera leo*) and a female tiger (*Panthera tigris*). The reverse cross produces a tigon.

2.  Wholphin: offspring of a cross between a male false killer whale (*Pseudorca crassidens*) and a female bottlenose dolphin (*Tursiops truncatus*).

3.  Cattalo: offspring of a cross between the North American buffalo (*Bison bison*) and cattle (*Bos* spp.).

4.  Mule: offspring of a cross between a male ass (donkey *Equus asinus*) and a horse (*Equus caballus*).

5.  Triticale (a grain crop): offspring of a cross of wheat (*Triticum*) and rye (*Secale*).

(Taken from 'Ligers and wholphins? What next?' by Don Batten (*Creation* **22**(3):28-33), found at www.AnswersInGenesis.org/liger.)

After Adam finished naming the animals God had brought to him, he probably realized that there was none like him. God put Adam to sleep, made Eve from his rib and brought her to him. This was the first marriage. Because all humans are descended from Adam (including Eve, who was made from Adam's rib), we are all related! Adam and Eve were the only part of God's creation made in His own image. (See 'Naming the animals: all in a day's work for Adam,' <www.AnswersInGenesis.org/docs/1254.asp>.)

## ♦ Read Genesis 1:27-31.

The creation of all things (including dinosaurs) took place only about 6,000 years ago. It was a perfect place. Adam and Eve had complete fellowship with God and lived in harmony with the rest of the creation. We cannot imagine what such a place would be like, but God tells us it was 'very good.' Adam, Eve and the animals were given plants to eat—this means that something like a *T. rex* was originally vegetarian.

## ♦ Read Genesis 2:2-4.

**Day 7:** God finished creating and rested. He continues to uphold and sustain His creation, however.

Now that your students understand God's eyewitness account of Creation, enable them to see the 'big picture' in understanding the real world. Reconnect this true account to the real world of

- Biology: The Bible explains that God created all things 'very good' (Genesis 1) but that the whole of Creation is under a curse (Genesis 3) due to Adam's disobedience. As you teach these passages, explain that while we expect to see marvelously designed features throughout the world (see <www.Answers InGenesis.org/design> for some examples), we also realize that these things are merely remnants of a once-perfect creation (due to the *Corruption* that entered the world—see next lesson).

- Astronomy: The Bible touches on astronomical concepts in many passages (beginning with Genesis 1) and provides a proper framework for studying the stars. There are even

Biblical principles that help address questions about 'life in outer space' (see <www.AnswersInGenesis.org/alien> for more information).

## ◆ Discussion questions

1. If God created dinosaurs on Day 6, when did He create dinosaur-like creatures such as pterodactyls or plesiosaurs?

   Day 5.

2. How do we know the Days of Creation were regular-length days and not thousands or millions of years?

   The Hebrew word for 'day' (*yom*) can have a variety of meanings, depending on its context. However, when it is used with the words 'evening' and/or 'morning' or with a number (i.e. one, two, etc.), it means a regular-length day. This is how the word 'day' is used in Genesis 1. List all the times these words are used in Genesis 1. (See <www. AnswersInGenesis.org/days> for more information.)

3. When did dinosaurs first appear on Earth?

   On the Sixth Day of Creation, about 6,000 years ago—not millions of years before humans.

## ◆ Activity ideas

1. Research some 'creation stories' of other cultures. How are they different from, or similar to, the *true* account found in Genesis?

2. Put together a 'Days of Creation' booklet. Have the students draw pictures of the major events of each day. Or visit <www. AnswersInGenesis.org/drawing> and <www.AnswersInGenesis. org/drawing2> for instructions on drawing the Days of Creation.

## ◆ If you have time …

If you have additional time, read 'What is the difference?' on the second page of the student handout, and go over the 'games' on the back page of the handout.

### ♦ Additional recommended reading

*A is for Adam*

*D is for Dinosaur*

*Dinosaurs of Eden*

*The Updated and Expanded Answers Book*

*Dinosaur cards*, available from *Answers in Genesis*

'The Seven C's of History' (Creation, Corruption, Catastrophe, Confusion, Christ, Cross, Consummation) help us remember the big events which have affected—and will affect—the history of the universe.

'In the beginning God created the heavens and the earth' (Genesis 1:1).

The first 'C' is the Creation of all things. In the Book of Genesis (which means 'beginnings'), God tells us He created everything in Six Days.

Let's take a quick look at what happened on each of those Six Days.

**Day 3**—God causes the waters under the expanse to come together, so that dry ground appears. Then He tells the land to bring forth plants and trees.

**Day 6**—God creates the land animals, including the dinosaurs, and—His most special creation—humanity. Adam and Eve are the first people—the great, great, great ... grandparents of us all! God gave them—and the animals—plants to eat.

When God had completely finished creating, He labeled all He had done as 'very good.' What would a 'very good' creation be like? Imagine a place with no death, no violence, no disease, no sickness, no thorns, no fear. Sounds like a great place to live!

**Day 1**—God says, 'Let there be light' and there is! He separates the light from the darkness and calls the light 'Day' and the darkness 'Night.' This light comes from a source other than the sun—the sun isn't created until Day 4.

**Day 4**—God makes the sun, the moon and the stars. These are to serve as signs to mark seasons, days and years. The sun and moon will rule the day and night, which cycle began on Day 1.

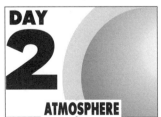

**Day 2**—God makes an expanse (something 'stretched out,' like a space) and separates the waters above the expanse from the waters below.

**Day 5**—God creates the animals which live in water and those which fly in the air.

**Day 7**—God 'rests'—or stops—His work of creation. Now He keeps upholding His creation (Col. 1:17).

God created all things in Six Days and rested on the Seventh. This became the first 'week.' Today, we follow this example by working for six days and resting for one!

# What is the difference

## between the two piles of wood below?

Of course, one pile of wood has been built into a tree house, while nothing has been done to the second pile of wood. Now, we all know that the first pile didn't organize itself. Rather, someone used the information from a drawing to build the wood into something you can play in!

Just as a blueprint was used to plan the assembly of the wood into a tree house, so a 'blueprint' is used in our bodies to plan the many complex systems that make us who we are. Our blueprint is called deoxyribonucleic acid (or DNA for short!). DNA stores the information needed to build our cells.

Science has shown that information can come only from intelligence. In the story above, the blueprints containing the information needed to build the tree house were drawn from the ideas of the designers. Where, then, did the information found in our cells come from?

## In the beginning, matter...

There are those who say all things (living and non-living) came from an explosion of matter (stuff that we're made of) billions of years ago. Over time, this matter supposedly organized itself into the many complex living creatures we see today—such as a blue jay or a daisy. However, we've seen that science has shown the matter cannot rearrange into high-information structures by itself.

Since the information in our DNA (which is far more complex than the information on the tree-house blueprint) can only come from a source of greater information (or intelligence), there must have been something other than matter in the beginning.

## In the beginning, God!

This 'other source' must have no limit to its intelligence—in fact, it must be an ultimate source o intelligence from which all things have come. The Bible tells us there is such a source—God. Sin God has no beginning and no end and knows all (Psalm 147:5), it makes sense that God is the source of the information we see all around us! This fits with real science, just as we would expe

There are those who say the first few chapters in Genesis are merely fairy tales with some truth.  However, since God is 'all-knowing' and since He wrote the original Book of Genesis, He should know how and when He created.  He says 'six days,' so it must be 'six days'!

Which of the following creatures have been on the Earth the longest?

A
B
C
D

ANSWER: A,C & D have been around the longest! All created on Day 5. (GENESIS 1:20-23) All land animals (including dinos) were created on Day 6! (GENESIS 1 24-31)

## DO YOU KNOW YOUR BIBLE?

Which of the Ten Commandments tells us God created the heavens and the Earth in 6 Days?

1.
2.
3.
4.

5.
6.
7.
8.
9.
10.

ANSWER: Commandment #4 Exodus 20:8-11

## LET THERE BE FUN!

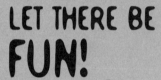

### Creation Days word scramble

These numbers stand for the Six Days of Creation. Each of the scrambled words relates to the Creation Day it is found in. See if you can unscramble each word!

THIGL

TWERA

WORSLEF

STEER

PEMAROTSEH

DANL

UNS

SEHAWL

ABSER

ROPSATR

SEAP

TASLEPN    RASTS

KRASHS

ROSIDANSU

CEMI

BSTA

SERSOH

LOPEEP

NOMO

SOPLISRAUSE

ANSWER: 1. LIGHT 2. WATER, ATMOSPHERE 3. FLOWERS, TREES, LAND 4. SUN, PLANETS, STARS, MOON 5. WHALES, PARROTS, SHARKS, BATS, PLESIOSAURS 6. BEARS, APES, DINOSAURS, MICE, HORSES, PEOPLE

# *Corruption*

## To obey or not to obey

**Text:** Genesis 2:15-17; Genesis 3–4
**Memory verse:** Genesis 2:17

We learned last week that God created all things in Six Days and rested on the Seventh. This is why we have seven days in our week. When God was finished creating, He declared all things 'very good.' But we don't see a 'very good' world today—rather, we live in a world filled with suffering and pain. The beautifully designed features of various animals are sometimes used to kill, or they're used as camouflage from an enemy—these post-Corruption 'struggle-for-survival' functions were not evident, as such, in God's original 'very good' world.

(Perhaps you could encourage your students to consider how various animal 'design' features function in today's (fallen) world, e.g. the sharp teeth of (formerly vegetarian) bears are now used for chewing meat, as well as bark, nuts, fruit, etc.)

Today's lesson reveals what happened to change the original paradise into the world we experience today.

### ◆ Read Genesis 2:15-17; 3:1-7.

We don't know how long Adam and Eve were in the Garden before the serpent came to tempt Eve, but it was probably only a few days. Adam and Eve were told to 'be fruitful and multiply,' so they would not have waited to carry out this command. Yet all of Eve's children were born sinners (Romans 5:12, 18-19), so she had not conceived in her sinless state.

To reiterate the Bible passage you just read, read 'Corruption,' the first page of this week's handout.

Adam and Eve (and thus, all of us, as descendants of Adam and Eve) chose not to listen to God's words. Instead, Eve was deceived into listening to the serpent's words, which changed what God had said into what the serpent wanted her to hear. Adam chose to disobey the very command of God *not* to eat from a certain tree in the middle of the Garden. This sin *corrupted* everything in God's perfect creation. Adam and Eve lost the close fellowship they had with their Creator, and his body began immediately to die.

*Corruption: changed from good to bad; spoiled; ruined

### ◆ Read Genesis 3:8-24.

To reiterate the Bible passage you just read, read 'Mirror, Mirror' (the second page of this week's handout), which highlights the effects of Adam's sin.

Complete obedience is very important to our holy God. Adam's one act of rebellion towards God's Word was so serious that it caused the entire universe to change. Because we (as children of Adam) choose to disobey as well, we need someone to take away our sin in order for us to spend eternity with God.

### ◆ Read Genesis 3:15 again.

God promised Adam and Eve that He would one day send a Savior to conquer sin. Do you know who that is? Jesus Christ.

Read 'Good enough *isn't* good enough!' to emphasize the point that we are all sinners in need of a Savior, and that nobody can be 'good enough' to get into Heaven on his own merit.

Now that your students understand why death and suffering are in the world, use this knowledge to explain:

- Why nature programs often feature violent scenes, such as lions ripping into zebras for their food. (Perhaps play a video clip of such a program for your students, if they are old enough to handle it.) This type of behavior (i.e. eating meat for food) would *not* have been part of God's original Creation but happens today because of sin's corruption.

- Why a loved one (or a pet) had to die. Death had no part in the original creation. Adam's sin (and ours) introduced death into the 'very good' world.

- The 'design' that we see in nature, although perhaps beautiful and reflective of the Creator, has been thoroughly tainted by sin. This explains why we see snakes using their fangs to kill prey, for example.

We don't know exactly *how* things changed into what we see today, though we know that being 'subjected to frustration ... by the will of the one who subjected it' has left the whole creation in 'bondage to decay,' suffering the downhill effects (e.g. genetic copying mistakes) of the Curse (Romans 8:20–22). Though the Lord holds all things together (Colossians 1:17), perhaps God partially withdrew his all-sustaining power after the Fall (cf. Israelite clothes and sandals in Deuteronomy 8:4; 29:5; Nehemiah 9:21—possibly an insight into pre-Fall conditions in Eden and in the future 'new heavens and new earth'). (See *The Updated and Expanded Answers Book* and <www.AnswersInGenesis.org/curse> for more information.)

## ◆ Read Genesis 4:1-17. ◆

Adam's son, Cain, committed the first murder; and Cain and his wife (who was either his sister or another close female relative) fled to another part of the world, away from his family. Unlike today, brothers and sisters married and had children with each other in the very beginning. This was not a problem at that time since

1. Adam and Eve were perfect, with no genetic mistakes. The first generation of children would have inherited relatively few mutations from their parents, and would have been able to marry freely (provided it was one man for one woman for life) with their close relatives, without worrying that their children would inherit serious defects. Today, 6,000 years after the Curse, genetic mistakes have accumulated generation after generation, so that each of us now carries many mutations in our genes. If close relatives were permitted to marry today, there would be many more offspring with serious defects. But when husband and wife are only distantly related (note: we are *all* distantly related, through Noah), they tend to have *different* copying mistakes, so the hope is that the children inherit at least one 'good' copy of each gene.

2. 'Incest' is a modern word describing a variety of actions, some of which have always been sinful, although not brother-sister marriage originally. The Biblical laws against brother-sister marriage were instituted around 2,000 years *after* Adam—during the time of Moses (Leviticus 18). These laws also forbade marrying one's half-sibling, but about 400 years earlier, Abraham was still able to marry his half-sister, Sarah, without breaking any law of God.

   *See 'Where did Cain get his wife?' <www.AnswersIn Genesis.org/cains_wife> for more information.

## ◆ Read Genesis 4:18-22.

Our early ancestors were not 'primitive,' as many believe. Adam immediately knew how and what to name all the animals, and his children farmed animals, grew crops and even built a city! Adam, who died at 930 years of age when Lamech (ninth from Adam via Seth) was over 60 years old, would almost certainly have still been alive when people had learned to work with metals (e.g. Tubal-Cain, eighth generation from Adam via Cain) and to play musical instruments.

## ◆ Discussion questions

1. How would you answer a friend who is seeking an explanation for all the violence present in our society today?

2. Compare Genesis 2:16–17 and Genesis 3:3–4. How did Eve change the Word of God when she responded to the serpent? What do Deuteronomy 4:2; 12:32; Proverbs 30:6 and Revelation 22:18–19 have to say about adding to or taking away from God's Word?

## ◆ Activity idea

Read *When Dragons' Hearts Were Good* to introduce the idea that 'dragons' could actually have been dinosaurs.

## ◆ If you have time …

End with the 'Did you know …' page.

## ◆ Additional recommended reading

*The Updated and Expanded Answers Book*

'Q&A: Genesis-Curse,' <www.AnswersInGenesis.org/curse>

'The Seven C's of History' (Creation, Corruption, Catastrophe, Confusion, Christ, Cross, Consummation) help us remember the big events which have affected—and will affect—the history of the universe.

'... but you shall not eat of the tree of knowledge of good and evil. For in the day that you eat of it you shall surely die' (Genesis 2:17).

We've seen that in the beginning God created the heavens and the Earth and everything was very good (Genesis 1–2). The next 'C,' Corruption, found in Genesis 3, is sad.

### From perfection ...

For a while, things were perfect in the Garden of Eden. Adam and Eve lived in a beautiful garden (planted especially for them by God) and could eat of any tree in Eden, except one. This first couple had a perfect relationship with their Creator, a perfect marriage and a perfect place to live. The animals, which Adam ruled over, got along perfectly. Something has obviously corrupted this 'very good' world into the world we see today, which is full of sickness and death.

### To imperfection ...

Adam and Eve both knew they could eat from any tree in the Garden of Eden except the one known as the Tree of the Knowledge of Good and Evil. God had forbidden them to eat of it, telling them that they would surely begin to die (the Hebrew in Genesis actually says, 'dying, you shall die') the very day they ate of it.

The devil, who took the form of a serpent, knew what God had said, but he caused Eve to question God's words by asking, 'Did God say you weren't to eat of any tree of the garden?' and then lying, 'You won't really die.' Eve believed the serpent, rather than God, and ate the forbidden fruit. Then she gave some to Adam, who hadn't been deceived by the serpent but ate it willingly (1 Tim. 2:14). This caused them both to immediately die spiritually (be separated from God) and to begin to die physically.

Because of his disobedience (sin), all of his descendants (this includes you and me!) are born with sin in our nature. Because of Adam's sin, our bodies will die. Because of Adam's sin, God cursed His precious creation. The world we see today, while reflecting God's original creation, has been corrupted by sin.

### To perfection ...

The good news of this sad tale is that God did not abandon His creation after Adam's sin! He promised that one day He would send a Savior, the 'seed of a woman' to bruise the head of the serpent (Genesis 3:15). This Savior, Jesus Christ, was indeed born of a woman without a human father, about 4,000 years later. He died on the Cross, and rose again to save His people from their sins, so indeed dealing a death-blow to (bruising the head of) the devil (serpent).

# Mirror Mirror

When we examine God's world, it's important to keep in mind that what we see today is only a dim reflection of God's perfect creation. The corruption that came through Adam's disobedience in the Garden of Eden changed God's handiwork completely. The effects of the Curse that God placed on His creation can be seen in various ways throughout our lives.

**For instance, have you ever asked yourself why ...**

**... those we love get sick and die?** God warned Adam that if he ate of the forbidden fruit, he would die. Romans 5:12 tells us that Adam's sin (and our sin through Adam) causes us all to die.

**... we get pricked by thorns when we try to smell a rose?** Because of Adam's disobedience, God cursed the ground, causing thorns and thistles to come from it (Genesis 3:18). Not only is the ground cursed, but Romans 8:22 tells us '... the whole creation groans and travails in pain together until now.'

**... we wear clothes?** After Adam sinned, he and Eve covered themselves with fig leaves, but man cannot cover sin. God killed an animal and used the skins to clothe Adam and Eve.

**... our parents have to work hard to provide for us?** Genesis 3:19 tells us God's Curse on man was that he must work hard to feed his family. In many countries, millions of people have to toil endlessly to provide just the basic necessities.

**... we don't all live in the Garden of Eden today?** Adam and Eve had to leave their home in the Garden so that they would not eat of the Tree of Life and live forever (Genesis 3:23). God did not want them to live forever in sin, separated from Him.

As terrible as things like pain, sickness and death are, they are not permanent parts of God's creation. We look forward to the last 'C' of History—Consummation—when the Curse will be no more (Revelation 22:3) and those whose names have been written in the Lamb's Book of Life will spend eternity in a perfect place.

# Good enough isn't good enough!

Because God is holy, His standard is perfection (Matthew 5:48). Because we sin, we are unable to work our way to Heaven (Romans 3:23). Eternal life is a gift offered by God (Ephesians 2:8-9) to those who realize they are sinners and are in need of a Savior, who is Jesus Christ (Romans 6:23). Jesus Christ died on the Cross and rose from the grave to pay for sin and to purchase a place in Heaven for those who turn from their sin and believe on Him (Isaiah 53 & John 3:16).

31

## DID YOU KNOW...

**Fossilized thorns have been found?**

Psilophyton crenulatum

Many claim these fossils are millions of years old. Does this fit with what we find in the Bible? Since fossils don't come with age-tags attached, it's impossible to know precisely how old they are. Since the Bible tells us thorns entered the world after God cursed the ground because of Adam's disobedience, these plants were fossilized after Adam sinned—not millions of years before.

HOLY BIBLE

## DO YOU KNOW YOUR BIBLE?

Does the Bible say the forbidden fruit was an apple?

**Answer:** No. The forbidden fruit is only referred to as a 'fruit.' The Bible doesn't tell us what kind of fruit it was.

## LET THERE BE FUN!

## Who said it?

Below are seven quotes found in Genesis 1-11.
See if you can match the quotes with who said them!

**A** GOD

**B** ADAM

**C** THE SERPENT

**D** EVE

**1** 'I do not know. Am I my brother's keeper?'

**2** 'Blessed be the LORD God of Shem, and Canaan shall be his servant ...'

**3** 'This is now bone of my bones and flesh of my flesh.'

**4** 'Let us make man in our image, after our likeness.'

**5** 'But of the fruit of the tree which is in the middle of the garden, God has said, You shall not eat of it, neither shall you touch it, lest you die.'

**6** 'Come, let us build us a city and a tower, and its top in the heavens.'

**7** 'You shall not surely die, for God knows that in the day you eat of it, then your eyes shall be opened ...'

**E** CAIN

**F** NOAH

**G** PEOPLE AT BABEL

**ANSWERS:**
A-4, B-3, C-7,
D-5, E-1, F-2,
G-6

## *Catastrophe*

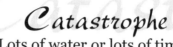

Lots of water or lots of time?

c. 2348 BC

**Text:** Genesis 6-9:19
**Memory verse:** Genesis 7:23

Many people believe that the vast number of sedimentary rock layers containing fossils found around the world formed over more than 500 million years. They believe that dinosaurs died out many millions of years before humans appeared on Earth. However, the Biblical record of history makes it clear that the Earth has only existed for a few thousand years. Therefore, these rock layers must have formed within this time frame, i.e. within the past few thousand years. The Earth-covering *Catastrophe* discussed in this lesson provides a basis for reconnecting the Bible to the real world of fossils and rock layers.

You may want to begin by reading 'Catastrophe' (from the student handout) or 'Noah: the man who trusted God,' <www.AnswersIn Genesis.org/noah_account>.

## ◆ Read Genesis 6:1-18; 7:1-7.

Before the Flood, there may have been just one landmass, rather than many continents as we see today, so there would have been no problems with animals migrating to the Ark from far distances. It was God (Noah didn't have to run around collecting all the animals) who brought two representatives (seven of the 'clean animals') of the various kinds of land animals that breathe through their nostrils, as well as flying creatures (Genesis 6:19-20; 7:2-3), to the Ark. There could well have been only about 16,000 individual animals in all—including dinosaur representatives! The Ark—able to hold the equivalent of 522 boxcars (rail freight wagons)—was quite big enough to hold all these animals, plus their food. Noah didn't have to take sea creatures.

> Note: The animals God brought to Noah were most likely 'teenagers' or younger—not fully grown. This applies to the dinosaur kinds on the Ark as well—younger, smaller dinosaurs would have easily been able to fit on the Ark.

## ◆ Read Genesis 7:11, 17-24.

The water for the globe-drenching Flood came from two sources: the 'fountains of the great deep' (possibly oceanic and/or subterranean sources of water) and the 'floodgates of the sky' (Genesis 7:11). As the waters increased, covered and later abated on the Earth, they picked up and carried vast amounts of different types of sediments (sand, gravel, lime, etc.), depositing these sediments over the face of the Earth, and burying many sea-dwelling, land-dwelling and air-dwelling creatures in the process. Nothing remains of that original Earth (2 Peter 3:8)—everything was destroyed, including the Garden of Eden. Many of the huge formations of rock (covering many square miles) and many fossils that we see today were laid down during the Flood. In fact, many of the rock layers that we can see exposed at the Grand Canyon were most likely formed during the Flood, while the canyon itself was carved in a later event.  The Earth's original geography would have been completely altered by the huge earth movements during the Flood.  According to leading creation scientists, it was during the Flood that the original landmass broke apart and the resulting continents shifted into the positions we find them today.  (See 'Probing the Earth's deep places,' <www.AnswersInGenesis.org/probing> for more information.)

## ◆ Read Genesis 8:1-3; Psalm 104:7–8.

These passages seem to indicate that at the end of the Flood the ocean basins sank down and mountains rose up.  (Interestingly, the tops of many of today's mountains (including Mt Everest) are composed of sedimentary rocks containing fossils, confirming that at one time they, too, were under water.)

Massive erosion would have occurred as the Flood waters drained off the land and into the ocean basins.

Biblical history makes it clear—it was 'lots of water' that made the Earth's topography what we see today, not 'lots of time'!

Read 'Thinkin' About Fossils!' with your students.  If you have your own fossils, this would be a good time to bring them in and let the students handle them.

## ◆ Read Genesis 8:4-9:7.

After the Ark was emptied, God permitted humans to eat meat for food (Genesis 9:3), and He placed the fear of man into the animals (Genesis 9:2).

While evolutionists and other long-agers have great difficulty accounting for any Ice Age, the global Flood and its aftermath provided the warm oceans (heated by volcanic activity and hot 'springs of the great deep') and cooler continents (from suspended volcanic ash/dust shading the Earth) necessary to generate the vast ice sheets that once covered extensive areas of our present-day continents (evidenced by remnant glaciers and u-shaped valleys).

High evaporation rates from warm seas would have generated huge clouds, which, if blown over a cold landmass, would cause water to precipitate as snow rather than rain. The accumulating snow on land would turn to ice, thus beginning the Ice Age, which may have lasted approximately 700 years and peaked about 500 years after the Flood. The ocean levels would have been lower during this time (possibly as much as 150 ft (45 m) lower than today's levels), as water was stored on land as snow and ice. With lower ocean levels, more land surface was exposed and land bridges were available for animals and people to eventually migrate all over the Earth. This harsh climate would have made it difficult for many animals to survive, however, thus causing their extinction.

(See <www.AnswersInGenesis.org/iceage> for more information.)

## ◆ Read Genesis 9:8-17.

Some people believe the Flood of Noah's day was just a local event, concentrated in a certain area. However, in this passage, God promises to never again flood the Earth as He did during Noah's day. If the Flood were only local, then God would have repeatedly broken His promise never again to send such a flood, because the Earth has experienced many localized floods since that time.

(See 'Noah's Flood covered the whole Earth,' <www.AnswersIn Genesis.org/global> for more information.)

## ◆ Read Genesis 6:14-17 again.

Many pictures of the Ark portray it as an overcrowded boat with animals hanging off its sides or out the windows, lending credence to the idea that this account is only a myth. However, the Bible gives a far different description of Noah's Ark. 'That's not the ark ... THIS is the Ark!' highlights the importance of portraying the Ark properly, according to Biblical dimensions, rather than furthering the idea that this account is just a 'fairy tale.'

## ◆ Discussion questions

1. Why did God judge the entire Earth during Noah's day?

Because of the sin of mankind.

2. How do we know the Flood covered the whole Earth?

    (See 'Noah's Flood covered the whole Earth,' <www.Answers InGenesis.org/docs/4104.asp>.)

3. What types of animals were with Noah on the Ark?

    (See 'Let there be fun!')

## ◆ Activity ideas

1. Use string to mark off the dimensions of the Ark: 450 ft long, 75 ft wide, 45 ft high (about 137 m long, 23 m wide and 13.7 m high).  Tie a helium-filled balloon to a string 45 ft (13.7 m) long and allow it to float to show how tall the Ark was.

2. Research some of the 'flood legends' found around the world— how are they similar to, or different from, the true account in Genesis?

3. Construct a time line of events during the Flood, showing how long it rained, how long the Flood waters were on the Earth, how long Noah and his family were on the Ark, etc.  (See Genesis 6-9 for help.)

## ◆ If you have time ...

Review this lesson by reading 'Catastrophe!' and the 'Did you know ... ?' pages.

## ◆ Additional resources

*The Updated and Expanded Answers Book*

*Life in the Great Ice Age*

*Dry Bones and Other Fossils*

*Noah's Ark: A Feasibility Study*

'Q&A: Flood,' <www.AnswersInGenesis.org/flood>

'Q&A: Noah's Ark,' <www.AnswersInGenesis.org/noah>

'Q&A: Plate Tectonics,' <www.AnswersInGenesis.org/tectonics>

'The Seven C's of History' (Creation, Corruption, Catastrophe, Confusion, Christ, Cross, Consummation) help us remember the big events which have affected—and will affect—the history of the universe.

'And every living thing which was on the face of the earth was destroyed, from man to cattle, and to the creeping things, and the fowls of the heavens. And they were destroyed from the earth, and only Noah was left, and those that were with him in the ark' (Genesis 7:23).

God created a perfect world in six normal-length days (Genesis 1–2), but Adam disobeyed God's command not to eat the forbidden fruit and brought corruption and death into the world (Romans 5:12). Adam's sin passed to his children, his children's children and so on. This brings us to the third 'C' of history found in Genesis 6-9 ...

As time went by, people began to invent new machines, explore new places, try new ideas.

Because their hearts were wicked, though, they did things that displeased their Creator. They didn't listen to their ancestor Adam as he told them what had happened in the Garden of Eden and how they needed to obey and worship only the Lord. This grieved God so much that He determined to destroy everything with the breath of life in it. Only one man, Noah, found favor in His eyes. God told Noah that He would send a great flood to judge the entire globe by covering it with water.

## Lions and tigers and ... dinosaurs?

Because the Creator knew Noah was a righteous man, God provided a way for him, his wife, his three sons, their wives, the land animals and birds (the fish and other sea creatures could survive in the water) to survive this catastrophe by building an ark. Noah and his family worked on the Ark for many years, probably warning those around them about God's judgment that was coming. Nobody but his family believed. When they finished building, God brought two of every animal (including dinosaurs!), and seven of some, to the Ark.

## And the rains came down ...

After all were on board, the 'windows of heaven' opened and the 'fountains of the great deep' broke up. These provided the water that would cover every spot on the whole Earth.

We've all seen the damage a local flood can do—ripping up trees, depositing layers of mud, destroying everything in its path. Now imagine the damage done by a flood covering the entire planet!

Nothing would be the same after the waters had left and the Earth had dried. How strange everything must have looked to Noah and his family as they came off the Ark!

After leaving the Ark, Noah built an altar to the Lord, sacrificing one of each of the clean animals. The Lord saw the sacrifice and promised to never flood the entire Earth again. The sign of this promise is the rainbow.

# Thinkin' about fossils!

Some scientists spend their whole lives studying the petrified remains of dead things (fossils) to try to understand what life was like in the past. This can be a fascinating job as these 'paleontologists' seek to determine when the animals (or plants, etc.) died, what they looked like while they were alive, how they moved, what they ate … . Each paleontologist looks at a fossil with certain ideas about what the past was like. In fact, we all do!

For instance, take a look at the fossil at the left. Now take a moment and write down, say, five things you know about that fossil.

Perhaps you said 'it's millions of years old,' or 'it took a long time to form.' Now think about what you've written for a moment—do you really know these things or are they just your ideas about the fossil? How do you know how old the fossil is or how long it took for the animal to be fossilized?

It's important, as Christians, that our ideas about the past are based on what the Bible tells us has happened. Using the Bible's true record of history to help us understand, we might say the following things about the fossil:

1. This animal died. Animal death was not a part of God's original creation, so the animal must have died after the world was corrupted through Adam's sin.
2. The fossil can't be 'millions of years' old since adding up the years in the Bible shows us the world is only a few thousand years old.
3. An animal that is buried quickly is more likely to be preserved than to decay and fall apart. The worldwide flood in Noah's day provided great conditions for quickly burying lots of animals and plants, so the animal may have died at this time (or in smaller local catastrophes which followed).

## These are just a few things we can learn from the Bible about this fossil.

Studying the fossils you find (maybe even in your own backyard!) can be exciting, but it's important to distinguish between what we actually find and what others may say about our findings. Since God's Word gives us the history of the world, we need to apply this to fossils as well.

# That's not the Ark ... THIS is the ARK!

Do the differences between these two drawings of Noah's Ark really matter?

**1** Look at what the Bible says about the shape of the Ark.

CUTE ARK PLANS

... the length of the ark shall be three hundred cubits, the breadth of it fifty cubits, and the height of it thirty cubits.
Genesis 6:15

HOLY BIBLE

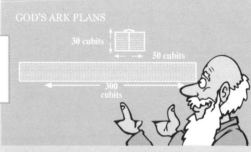

GOD'S ARK PLANS

30 cubits
50 cubits
300 cubits

**2** The Ark must float.

This type of boat will tip over easily in rough water.

God designed the Ark to stay upright in the violent storms and huge waves of a global flood.

AAAAAAAAAAAAA AII!!

**3** It must be BIG!

Most 'arks' look tiny and over-crowded.

The real Ark had the same capacity as 522 railroad stock cars! It had lots of room.

Ham, move over!

OUCH! That hurt!

Shem, get off my foot!

You believe in that? HA HA HA!

Why make Bible story pictures look like fairy tales? Too many people already think the Bible is impossible to believe.

2 Peter 3:5-6

Yes, Noah's Ark WAS real. In fact ...

Wow!

The next time you see one of these just remember what the Bible says!

## Did you know?

Water covers 70% of the Earth's surface? Yet many deny the Earth was completely covered in water at one time. Did you also know ... no (liquid) water has been found on Mars? Yet many believe water shaped the surface of the Red Planet (Mars) in the past. Why would people deny a huge flood on Earth and promote one on Mars?

2 Peter 3:5-6 reminds us, 'For this is hidden from them by their willing it, that ... the world that then was, being flooded by water, perished.'

## DO YOU KNOW YOUR BIBLE?
### Who closed the door to the Ark?

**Answer:** Genesis 7:16 'And they that entered, went in male and female of all flesh, as God had commanded him: and the LORD shut him in.'

## LET THERE BE FUN!

## All aboard Noah's Ark?

God told Noah to have at least two of certain kinds of animals (seven of some) on board the Ark (Genesis 6:19-7:3). The animals shown here in pairs were on the Ark. There are fifteen pairs for you to match. These animals *were* on the Ark. Ten of the animals shown here were not on the Ark because they could survive outside of it. These animals do not have a pair. Circle the animals that were not on the Ark!

Animals on the Ark: *Apatosaurus*, bat, bird (flying), dodo bird, giraffe, horse, kangaroo, mammoth, monkey, mouse, rabbit, rhinoceros, skunk, snake, *Tyrannosaurus rex*.

Animals not on the Ark: dolphin, eel, fish (gold), *Kronosaurus*, octopus, plesiosaur, sea horse, shark, starfish, whale.

# Confusion
We're all related!
c. 2247 BC

**Text:** Genesis 9:18-11:9
**Memory verse:** Genesis 11:7-8

Ever since Adam ate the fruit from the Tree of the Knowledge of Good and Evil, man has rebelled against the Word of his Creator. Rebellion continues to be the theme of the lives of the descendants of Noah and his family. And God, because He is holy and just, must continue to punish this sin. Approximately 100 years after the Flood of Noah's day, in 2347 BC, a group of people once again refused to listen to, and obey, the Word of God.

Read 'The land of Shinar 4,000 years ago,' the third page in this week's handout.

Where did all the so-called 'races' of people come from? Do any of you speak a language other than English? Why are there so many different kinds of language families? The Bible provides the 'big picture' so we can understand the answers to these (and other) questions.

♦ **Read Genesis 8:14-19; 11:1-9.**

God confused the language at Shinar so that the people would spread out and fill the Earth, as He had commanded them to. The language difference made it difficult for families to communicate, so they split apart, each family going their own way. (Today's languages have 'descended' from those original ones. While linguists today can group languages into 'families,' they are unable to find linkages that might trace all languages back to a single common ancestral language—exactly what we would expect from the Biblical account of confusion into distinct languages at Babel.)

The land bridges that formed as a result of the Ice Age enabled these families (and animals) to travel from Shinar to other parts of the world, such as what we know today as Australia or the Americas. They probably also used boats to travel across the seas (e.g. Pacific islanders).

Read 'Confusion!'—the first page of the handout, which explains the origin of the various 'people groups.'

Ask your students, 'How many of you have heard of "cave men"?' Read 'Cave man 101' from the handout with your students.

'Cave man 101' points out that the so-called 'cave men' were merely men (and their families) trying to make the best of their new situation with the capabilities they possessed. Evidence has been found of people living near the edge of the ice sheets in Western Europe. The small amount of sunlight, coldness and dampness in these areas probably contributed to various diseases (such as rickets and arthritis) that the people living there suffered. The Neanderthals were one such people group. Many anthropologists believe that the stooped, brute-like appearance of some Neanderthal skeletons was, at least partially, caused by these conditions.

Job probably lived between the time of Babel and Abraham. There seem to be indications in the book written about him that he experienced some effects (snow, ice, etc.) of what we know today as the Ice Age (Job 37:9-10; 38:22-23, 29-30).

Job also may have had encounters with animals we call dinosaurs. The word 'dinosaur' wasn't invented until 1841, so it wouldn't be found in literature written before this time. The Bible uses other words to describe dinosaur-like creatures. Job 40 mentions a creature called 'behemoth,' which was so large that his tail was like that of a cedar tree. This could possibly be referring to something like *Brachiosaurus!* And Job 41 mentions a water-dwelling creature, *Leviathan,* that may have been what we call *Kronosaurus* or *Liopleurodon.*

There are other accounts told throughout the world of 'dragons,' and many of the descriptions match those of the animals we know as 'dinosaurs.' Much historical evidence indicates that such creatures co-existed with man.

In the film *The Great Dinosaur Mystery* (Taylor, P., *The Great Dinosaur Mystery,* Films for Christ, Mesa, Arizona, 1991; see also the book: Taylor, P., *The Great Dinosaur Mystery and the Bible,* Accent Publications, Denver, Colorado, 1989) a number of dragon accounts are presented:

- A Sumerian story dating back to 2,000 BC or more tells of a hero named Gilgamesh, who, when he went to fell cedars in a remote forest, encountered a huge vicious dragon, which he slew, cutting off its head as a trophy.

- When Alexander the Great (c. 330 BC) and his soldiers marched into India, they found that the Indians worshipped huge hissing reptiles that they kept in caves.

- China is renowned for its dragon stories, and dragons are prominent on Chinese pottery, embroidery and carvings.

- England has its story of St George, who slew a dragon that lived in a cave.

- There is an account of a 10th-century Irishman who wrote of encountering what appears to have been a *Stegosaurus.*

- In the 1500s, a European scientific book, *Historia Animalium,* listed several animals that we would call dinosaurs, as still alive. A well-known naturalist of the time, Ulysses Aldrovandus, recorded an encounter between a peasant named Baptista and a dragon whose description fits that of the small dinosaur *Tanystropheus*. The encounter was on 13 May 1572, near Bologna in Italy, and the peasant killed the dragon.

Petroglyphs (drawings carved on rock) of dinosaur-like creatures have also been found.

(See 'Messages on stone,' <www.AnswersInGenesis.org/messages> for more information.)

## ♦ Discussion questions

1. If your family were suddenly cut off from the rest of civilization, what types of abilities would you have? Would you know how to build a brick home, or would you have to survive in caves or in houses made of wood? Would you know how to build a fire and kill and cook animals for food? Would you know how to make musical instruments or toys? Would you be able to make your own clothing?

2. Since we are all of 'one blood,' is there any such thing as 'interracial marriage'?

   No.

3. What is true 'interracial marriage'?

   When a child of the last Adam (a Christian) marries a child of the first Adam (a non-Christian)—2 Corinthians 6:14. See 'Interracial marriage: is it Biblical?' <www.AnswersIn Genesis.org/interracial>.

## ♦ Activity ideas

1. Bring to class a map that shows the extent of the Ice Age, and talk about the map with your students.

2. Research the 'cedars of Lebanon'—how large or small were they? How large would an animal's tail have to be in order to be compared to a cedar tree?

3. Some people believe the 'Tower of Babel' may have been something like a ziggurat. Research people groups that used ziggurats—what did these structures look like? What was their use? Why would many similar-looking structures be used by so many different people groups?

4. Draw a picture of 'behemoth,' based on Job 40.

5. Research other 'dragon' legends. Which ones do you think may have actually been based on encounters with dinosaurs?

## ◆ **If you have time …**

Conclude with the 'Let there be fun!' page.

## ◆ **Additional resources**

*The Updated and Expanded Answers Book*

*Great Dinosaur Mystery* (video)

*Great Dinosaur Mystery Solved!* (book)

*Puzzle of Ancient Man*

*Life in the Great Ice Age*

*Dinosaurs of Eden*

'Q&A: Racism, Origin of "Races," ' <www.AnswersInGenesis.org/racism>

'Q&A: Dinosaurs,' <www.AnswersInGenesis.org/dinosaurs>

CONFUSION

HELPING CHILDREN DEFEND THEIR FAITH

'The Seven C's of History' (Creation, Corruption, Catastrophe, Confusion, Christ, Cross, Consummation) help us remember the big events which have affected—and will affect—the history of the universe.

'Come, let us go down and there confuse their language, so that they cannot understand one another's speech. So the LORD scattered them abroad from that place upon the face of all the earth. And they quit building the city' (Genesis 11:7-8).

## In the beginning

God's perfect creation was corrupted by Adam's sin. During the days of Noah, God judged the wickedness of man with a great catastrophe, covering the entire planet with water.

After Noah and his family came off the Ark, God commanded them to spread out and fill the Earth (now very different from before the Flood). But the descendants of Noah disobeyed God.

They decided to stay in one place, building a tall tower, they hoped would help keep them all together.

When the Lord saw their disobedience, He was displeased—as He is with all disobedience—and He confused the language of the people so they couldn't understand each other (until this time, they all spoke one language).

In this way, the Creator scattered them over all the Earth.

The several different languages created suddenly at Babel (Genesis 10–11) could each subsequently give rise to many more. Language gradually changes, so when a group of people breaks into several groups which no longer interact, after a few centuries they may each speak a different (but related) language. Today, we have thousands of languages but fewer than 20 language 'families.'

## Back up a minute

Adam and Eve were the first humans. Then all humans died except Noah, his wife and their three sons and daughters-in-law during the Flood of Noah. If we're all descended from the same two people, then why do we look so different from each other?

## Creative differences

Actually, this 'C' has a lot to do with answering this question!

God created Adam and Eve with the ability to produce children with a variety of different characteristics. This ability was passed on through Noah and his family.

As the people scattered, they took with them different amounts of the information for certain characteristics—e.g. height, the amount of pigment for hair and skin color (we all have the same pigment, just more or less of it), etc.

From this one event, the tribes and nations of the world have resulted. Because we all came from Noah's family a few thousand years ago, we're all related!

# Cave man 101

## Where'd they come from?

'Cave men' supposedly lived thousands of years before 'modern man' came on the scene. But God, in His Word, tells us the true history of these people. In Genesis, He tells us that Adam and Eve were the first two people on Earth. Later, only Noah and his family were left on Earth after God judged man's disobedience with a worldwide Flood.

Then, after God *confused* the languages at Babel because of man's disobedience, various groups split up, taking with them their individual knowledge of technology. Some knew more about farming, some (such as those who were working on the Tower of Babel) knew more about building great structures, and some knew how to use metal to make tools. Those groups which didn't know how to do any of these things would be forced to 'begin again'—learning these skills on their own. Those who did have these skills were able to use them once they found a suitable place to settle—building great pyramids or magnificent gardens.

## Where'd they live?

Many families who weren't expert builders would have found caves a good place to quickly make new homes. Today, the people who lived in these caves are called 'cave men.' There was nothing 'primitive' about them, however—they used musical instruments, drew fascinating pictures on cave walls, knew how to make stone tools, could sew their own clothes and hunted their food with great skill. When their bones are found, they are similar to our bones, showing they really were people like us!

## Where do you live?

'In the brick house down the street on the right,' may be the answer you give to that question. Others may say they live in a house made of wood, or in a flat, or on a houseboat, or even underground. Are those who live in brick houses more intelligent than those who live underground? Absolutely not! These families simply live in different places, just as happened after Babel.

In fact, in Coober Pedy (in Australia), living above ground is very hot, so many people build their homes underground—real live 'cave men' with television sets!

## Who were they?

Evolutionists believe the evidence they find of those who lived in caves points toward us having less-than-human ances However, seeing these things through 'Biblical glasses' helps us rightly understand that these people were descendants Noah and were, in fact, our relatives!

# The Land of Shinar 4,000 years ago

### A story based on Genesis 11:1-9

Meet Joey and Ben. They are best friends.

Hi!

Welcome to Shinar.

Their fathers both work building a big new tower. A tower God doesn't want the people to build.

Is it done yet?

Not yet.

Coming soon!

God told the people to spread out and fill the Earth, but the people didn't listen and stayed in one spot.

My father says this tower means we will always be together.

!

Today, something is about to happen that will make the people move apart ...

Hey Joey, want to hear a joke?

Sure!

... Here it comes!

Knock, knock ...

Who's there?

Wate

Water who?

Quale vu nomesas?

??

God has just confused the language. Joey and Ben can't understand each other anymore.

Me ne komprenas.

?

Je ne comprends pas.

?

Instead of one language for the whole world, now there are many languages.

No te comprendo!

?   ?   ?

ჰო? გაგიგე

?   ?

Everything comes to a stop. Without the ability to communicate, it is hard to work together.

NAN TE iiMASHITAKA ???

?

WAS HAST DU GESAGT ???

?

¿Que dices?

?

En ymmärrä

Ek verstaan nie.

Ya ne ponimayu

Δεν καταλαβαίνω

?

Because each family group cannot understand the other groups, they move apart.

Joey and Ben wave goodbye, never to see each other again. It is a sad day.

WOW! that was some dream! I guess learning about the Tower of Babel in church really affected me.

Later that day

Hey, Al! last night I dreamed about the Tower of Babel. It was all so real.

There were two friends and when God confused the languages they ...

¿Que dices? No te comprendo!

!

OH NO! Al, I can't understand you!

HA HA! I just thought I'd practise some of the new words I learned in Spanish class!

Basic Spanish

Whew! it was like being at Babel again!

## DID YOU KNOW...

hundreds of 'flood legends' have been found throughout the world? In fact, most of today's people groups tell stories that sound very similar to what we read in Genesis. Why? It makes sense that, as the people split up after Babel, they took with them the tales their ancestors had passed on to them about the great catastrophe of Noah's day.

**The true account was preserved by God and written down by Moses so that all would remember what had happened and would learn to obey Him.**

## DO YOU KNOW YOUR BIBLE?

Does the Bible call the tower in Genesis 11:1-9 the 'Tower of Babel'?

**Answer:** No. Genesis 11:1-9 only refers to it as 'a tower.' However, it is called the Tower of Babel today because the city where the tower was built was called Babel.

## LET THERE BE FUN!

### Babel word scramble

Read Genesis 11:1-9, and then unscramble the words below to find out what they say.

1. EHLOW

2. RAHTE

3. PESKO

4. MEAS

5. NULEGAGA

6. SRODW

## Babel word find

The thirteen words listed below are hidden in the tower-shaped puzzle. Look forward, backward, up and down. See if you can find them all.

Shinar, people, sin, build, tower, bricks, city, God, language, confusion, Babel, scatter, Genesis

```
        SHINARN
       ODALNAD
      TEFTREWOT
     EDLBINMBABEL
    CAFVATYHUJIDASKEM
   SSCONFUSIONANIHFE
  OSKERFGOTMARCIANDUJIM
 AKCTHIUFGOBHRETTACSUN
AJEFGIJKLAERATGHGHBUILDNNG
AWLEDRFTIGENESISYGEBAICATS
YTICZBUJIEHOPEOPLEUNJIMGOD
```

Word Scramble
**ANSWERS:** 1. WHOLE 2. EARTH 3. SPOKE 4. SAME 5. LANGUAGE 6. WORDS

## *Christ*

God becomes a man

**Text:** Genesis 3:15; Matthew 1:1-25; Luke 1:26-2:40; John 1:1-14
**Memory verse:** Matthew 1:21-23

Who was Jesus Christ?  Just a good teacher?  A man of great morals?  An interesting philosopher?  Where did He come from?  What did He accomplish?  Jesus Christ is the central figure in history.  Yet most people don't understand the real reason He came to Earth or why He had to die.  They don't realize that His coming was all part of God's eternal plan.

### ◆ Read Genesis 3:15; Luke 1:26-38; 2:1-20.

Now read 'Christ' (the first page in this week's handout), looking up the verses as you come to them.

The life of Jesus the Messiah, the Creator-Redeemer, is recorded in four main books, which are part of the New Testament. The authors of these books were inspired by the Holy Spirit to record the events of Jesus' life.

### ◆ Read Matthew 1:1-17.

Have your students compare the names listed in the genealogy with those in the 'From Adam to Christ' chart. You will notice that there are more men listed in the chart than are in Matthew's list. The explanation: Matthew was a Jewish tax collector and one of the 12 disciples of Jesus (Matthew 9:9; 10:3). Careful study of Matthew's book reveals that he wrote primarily for a Jewish readership, as he documents the Old Testament prophecies that Jesus, as the Messiah, fulfilled. This fulfillment of prophecy would have been particularly interesting to a Jew. Matthew emphasizes the kingly nature of Jesus. He also shows that Jesus was descended from Abraham, the father of the Jews, through Joseph. Matthew's genealogy (1:1-17) from Abraham to Christ is intentionally incomplete—he selected just 3 groups of 14 men. There are other listings in the Old Testament which *are* complete, and which help fill in the known 'gaps' in Matthew's list (e.g. Genesis 5; Genesis 11; 1 Chronicles 3:11-12; 2 Kings 23:34; 2 Kings 24:6).

Mark was probably acquainted with Jesus because Mark's mother was the owner of the 'upper room' where the last supper between Jesus and His disciples took place. Mark's account of Jesus' life is thought to emphasize the servanthood of Jesus, and it was most likely written for Roman believers.

### ◆ Read Mark 5:21-42.

Remember that death, disease and sickness are not a permanent part of God's creation. They only came about after Adam sinned. In this passage, Jesus (the Creator God) shows His power over these things by healing Jairus' daughter and raising the daughter of the ruler of the synagogue from the dead.

(See also 'Walking trees ... modern science helps us understand a modern miracle,' <www.AnswersInGenesis.org/miracle>.)

Luke, the 'beloved physician,' addressed his account (and his second book, Acts) to a relatively unknown man, Theophilus, with an emphasis on the humanity of the Messiah.  Luke's genealogy (3:23-38) is different from Matthew's because Luke traces Jesus' heritage through His mother, Mary (rather than through His supposed earthly father, Joseph, as Matthew does).  Luke's genealogy extends back to the father of us all—Adam.

## ◆ Read Luke 3:23-38.

Compare the names given to those on the chart.

Here are a few reasons for understanding that it was Mary's lineage that Luke chose to present:

*   Luke's narrative mainly presents Mary's perspective, while Matthew presents Joseph's perspective.  So readers of the original Greek would realize that these two narratives were intended to present Mary's and Joseph's lines respectively.

*   Luke didn't mention Mary explicitly because rules for listing Jewish ancestry generally left out the mothers' names.

*   A clear pointer to the fact that Luke gives Mary's line is that he put a definite article before all the names *except* Joseph's.  Any Greek-speaker would have understood that Heli must have been the father of Joseph's *wife*.  Because the article is missing, the reader would insert the father's name, 'Joseph,' into the parenthesis '(as was supposed)' in Luke 3:23.  So he would *not* read the sentence as 'Jesus ... being (as was supposed) the son of Joseph, the son of Heli,' but as 'Jesus ... being son (as was supposed of Joseph) of Heli.'  (Note: the original Greek had no punctuation—or even spaces—between words.)  Indeed, the Jewish Talmud—no friend of Christianity—dating from the first few centuries AD, calls Mary the 'daughter of Heli,' which could

only be true if this is what Luke meant.

What about 'Cainan'?

> Luke (3:36) lists 'Cainan' as the father of Shelah and the son of Arphaxad, yet Cainan's name is not listed in the genealogy of Genesis 11:12. Some have used this to say the Bible itself is mistaken and fallible.

> We chose to omit this second 'Cainan' in our list from Adam to Christ because several lines of evidence would indicate that his inclusion was not part of the original, inspired manuscripts, but probably resulted from a copyist's error. As a scribe was copying Luke's Gospel, it is possible that he inadvertently added an extra Cainan as the father of Shelah.

> (For more information, please see 'Cainan: How do you explain the difference between Luke 3:36 and Genesis 11:12?' <www.AnswersInGenesis.org/cainan>.)

## ◆ Read John 1:1-5, 10-14.

John worked as a fisherman. He begins his book with the words 'In the beginning … ', showing the eternal and divine nature of the Word (Jesus Christ), as well as portraying Him as Creator (1:3).

## ◆ Discussion questions

1. What verses in the New Testament show Jesus Christ is the Creator God?

   > Matthew 1:23; John 14:9; Colossians 1:16. See also 'Is Jesus Christ the Creator God?' (<www.AnswersInGenesis.org/docs/3804.asp>).

2. What verses in the New Testament confirm that God created?

   > John 1:1-3; Colossians 1:15-17; Ephesians 3:9; Hebrews 1:1-3

3. Jesus fulfilled many more prophesies than the ones we've listed on the 'From Adam to Christ' chart. What other fulfilled prophecies can you find?

4. How many references in the New Testament can you find that refer to historical events described in Genesis?

> Matthew 19:5–6; 24:37-39; Mark 10:6-7; Luke 11:51; 17:26; Acts 17:24; Romans 5:12-19; 1 Corinthians 6:16; 11:8–9; 15:21, 45; 2 Corinthians 11:3; Ephesians 5:31; Colossians 1:16; 1 Timothy 2:13–14; Hebrews 1:10; 4:4, 10; 11:3–4; 1 Peter 3:20; 2 Peter 2:5; 3:5–6; Jude 11; Revelation 10:6; 20:2

## ◆ Activity ideas

1. Trace the route Joseph and his family probably took from Bethlehem to Egypt to Nazareth.

2. Research the gifts given by the Magi to Jesus. What were they? What were their uses?

## ◆ If you have time ...

Review this lesson by reading the 'Do you know your Bible?' page, and the 'Problem solved,' 'Special women' and 'Prophecies' boxes on the 'Adam to Christ!' chart.

## ◆ Additional resource

A.T. Robertson's *Harmony of the Gospels*

'The Seven C's of History' (Creation, Corruption, Catastrophe, Confusion, Christ, Cross, Consummation) help us remember the big events which have affected—and will affect—the history of the universe.

'And she shall bear a son and you shall call His name JESUS: for He shall save His People from their sins. Now all this happened so that might be fulfilled that was spoken of the LORD by the prophet, saying, "Behold, the virgin shall conceive in her womb, and will bear a son. And they will call His name Emmanuel," which being interpreted is, God with us' (Matthew 1:21–23).

God's perfect creation was corrupted by Adam when he disobeyed God. This disobedience brought sin and death into the world. Because of Adam's disobedience, and because we have all sinned personally anyway, we are all deserving of the death penalty and need a Savior (Romans 5:12).

God did not leave His precious—but corrupted—creation without hope. He promised to send Someone one day who would take away the penalty for sin, which is death (Genesis 3:15, Ezekiel 18:4, Romans 6:23).

God slew an animal in the Garden (a lamb/sheep?) because of the sin of Adam, so Adam's descendants sacrificed animals. Such sacrifices could only *cover* sin—they looked forward to the time when the ultimate sacrifice would be made by the One whom God would send (Hebrews 9).

When God gave Moses the Law, people began to see that they could never measure up to God's standard of perfection (Romans 3:20)—if they broke any part of the Law, the result was the same as breaking the whole lot (James 2:10)!

They needed Someone to take away their imperfection and present them faultless before God's throne (Romans 5:9, 1 Peter 3:18).

## God's gift to us

Just as God has a purpose and plan for everything and everyone, so He sent His promised Savior at just the right time (Galatians 4:4). There was a problem, however. All humans are descended from Adam, and therefore all humans are born with sin. God's chosen One must be perfect, as well as infinite, to take away the infinite penalty for sin.

God solved this 'problem' by sending His Son Jesus Christ—completely human and completely God. Think of it—the Creator of the universe (John 1:1-3, 14) became part of His creation so that He might save His people from their sins!

Jesus was born to a virgin over 2,000 years ago in a town called Bethlehem, as the prophets Isaiah (7:14) and Micah (5:2) had foretold 700 years previously. His parents took

Him to Egypt to escape the anger of King Herod, and the family later settled in Nazareth.

Jesus fulfilled more than 50 prophecies made about Him centuries before, showing He was the One promised over 4,000 years before by His Father. While He spent over 30 years on Earth, He never once sinned—He did nothing wrong. He healed many people, fed huge crowds and taught thousands of listeners about their Creator God and how to be reconciled to Him. He even used the Book of Genesis to explain that marriage is between one man and one woman (Matthew 19:3-6, quoting Genesis 1:27 and 2:24).

Jesus Christ came to Earth so that we might have eternal life with Him!

**CREATION**

C. 4004 BC

**Adam**

**CORRUPTION**

**CATASTROPHE**

 Seth

 Enos

 Cainan

 Mahalaleel

 Jared

 Enoch

 Methuselah

 Lamech

**Noah**

Flood
C. 2348 BC

 Shem

 Arphaxad

 Salah

When Adam disobeyed, the perfect fellowship he had enjoyed with his Creator was destroyed. God promised that one day, Someone would be born—a descendant of Adam—who would rescue His creation from the Curse that God had placed on it (Genesis 3:15). This person was Jesus Christ—the Messiah. This chart lists all the men who were descendants of Adam and ancestors of Jesus.

 Hezron

 Perez

 Judah

 Jacob

 Isaac

**Abraham**
C. 2000 BC
prophecy given in Gen. 21:12 that the promised One would come through Isaac

 Terah

 Nahor

 Serug

 Reu

 Peleg

Division at Babel in Peleg's day
C. 2247 BC

**CONFUSION**

 Eber

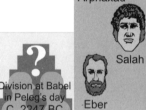

 Ram

Amminadab

Nahshon

Salmon

Boaz

Obed

Jesse

## Problem solved

God promised that David would always have a descendant on his throne (Jeremiah 23:15; 1 Chronicles 17:10-14). The legal right to this throne was passed through David's son, Solomon, to his descendants. Jeconiah (or Jehoiachin), a great, great ... grandson of Solomon and king of Judah, was so wicked that God punished him by declaring that none of his children would ever again sit on the throne (Jeremiah 22:17–30). This caused a 'problem' since Joseph, the supposed 'father' of Jesus, was a descendant of Jeconiah. If Joseph had been Jesus' *biological* father, Jesus would have had the *legal* right to the throne, but would have been unable to occupy it due to being under Jeconiah's curse. God solved this problem by using Mary: Jesus was the first-born son of Mary, a virgin (Matthew 1:23) and a descendant of David through another son, Nathan. So Jesus has the right to sit on the eternal throne of David—legally, through his adoptive father, Joseph; and physically, through His natural mother Mary. In this way, God's promise mentioned above in Jeremiah and Chronicles was fulfilled.

 Nathan

 Mattathah

 Menan

 Melea

 Eliakim

 Jonan

 Joseph

 Judah

 Simeon

 Levi

Matthat

**David**
C. 1000 BC

 Solomon

 Rehoboam

 Abijah

 Asa

 Jehoshaphat

 Jehoram

 Ahaziah

 Joash

 Amaziah

 Uzziah

 Jotham

 Ahaz

Heze...

Rhesa · Joannas · Judah · Joseph · Semei · Mattathiah · Maath · Naggai · Esli · Nahum · Amos · Mattathiah · Joseph

Janna

Zerubbabel · Shealtiel · Neri · Melchi · Addi · Cosam · Elmodam · Er · Joshua · Eliezer

Melchi · Levi · Matthat · Heli

**Mary**

**CHRIST**
C. 6 BC

## Special women

Matthew's list of people from Abraham to Christ mentions four women. Rahab was involved in a grossly immoral lifestyle before turning from her sins and trusting the true God, who is gracious to repentant sinners. Only one of the four (Bathsheba) was an Israelite. Nevertheless, God allowed all of them to be included in the ancestry of His son.

## Prophecies

The prophecies concerning the promised Messiah were made between 400 and 4,000 years before Jesus was born. A few of those prophecies are listed here, along with the places in Scripture indicating Jesus fulfilled these prophecies.

The Messiah would be:

- Born in Bethlehem—Micah 5:2; Matthew 2:1
- Presented with gifts—Psalm 72:10; Matthew 2:1, 11
- Called Lord (a reference to His deity)—Psalm 110:1; Luke 2:11
- Called 'Almighy God' and Father of Eternity—Isaiah 9:6; John 20:28
- Born of a virgin and called Emmanuel—Isaiah 7:14; Matthew 1:23; cf. Genesis 3:15
- Riding into Jerusalem on the foal of a donkey—Zechariah 9:9; Matthew 21:5
- Pierced in His hands and feet—Psalm 22:16; compare the whole Psalm with the details of crucifixion
- Killed 483 (69x7) years after the decree to rebuild Jerusalem—Daniel 9:24-27
- Thrust through—Zechariah 12:10; John 19:34
- Called a Prophet like Moses (i.e. who would receive face-to-face revelation from God the Father)—Deuteronomy 18:18-19; Matthew 21:11
- Called Priest—Psalm 110:4; Hebrews 3:1
- Preceded by a messenger (John the Baptist)—Isaiah 40:3; Matthew 3:1, 2

**Joseph**

Jacob · Matthan

Jorim

Manasseh · Josiah · Jeconiah · Shealtiel · Abiud · Azor · Achim · Eleazar
Amon · Jehoiakim · Zerubbabel · Eliakim · Zadok · Eliud

## DO YOU KNOW YOUR BIBLE?

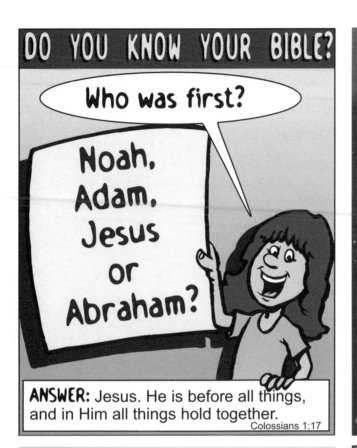

Who was first?

Noah,
Adam,
Jesus
or
Abraham?

**ANSWER:** Jesus. He is before all things, and in Him all things hold together.
Colossians 1:17

## What was Jesus' first miraculous act?

Many would answer 'turning water into wine' (John 2). However, the Apostle John says this is just the first sign that Jesus performed in His earthly ministry. The Bible actually records a miracle of Jesus that occurred over 4,000 years before He was even born. John began his Gospel by saying that Jesus, the Word, 'was God' and 'all things came into being through Him, and without Him not even one thing came into being that has come into being' (John 1:3). Paul tells us, 'For all things were created by Him ...' (Colossians 1:16).

The first miracle Jesus performed that the Bible tells about is that of Creation!

## Jesus the Christ

The list (on the inside pages) of people from Adam to Christ shows that Jesus was a human—a descendant of the first man, Adam. In fact, Jesus referred to Himself many times as the 'Son of Man' (e.g. Matthew 9:6; 12:40). The Bible also tells us that Jesus was God. John says, '... the Word [Jesus] was God' (John 1:1, 14). Paul calls Jesus 'our great God and Savior' (Titus 2:13), and Thomas refers to Him as 'my Lord and my God' (John 20:28). Many addressed Him as the 'Son of God' (John 11:27, etc.)—a name which Jesus also used about Himself (John 10:36). Matthew gives Him the title Emmanuel, which means 'God with us' (Matthew 1:23).

In addition, just as God did in the Old Testament, Jesus raised the dead (John 5:21; 1 Samuel 2:6), forgave sins (Matthew 9:2, 6; Jeremiah 31:34), and healed the sick (Luke 8:47; Exodus 15:26). As God, Jesus deserves our worship for who He is and what He has done for us (John 5:23).

## LET THERE BE FUN!

Each of the people in the answers is shown on the 'Adam to Christ' chart on the inside.

Jude 14 tells about a man who was the 'seventh from Adam.'

This man lived the longest—969 years!

He had 12 children who became the leaders of the 12 tribes of Israel.

This king reigned the longest of any king of Judah—55 years.

This man led the captive Jews back to Palestine in 536 BC under the permission of Cyrus, King of Persia.

This king was struck with leprosy because of his disobedience toward God at the end of his reign.

**Answers:** A. Enoch B. Methuselah C. Jacob D. Manasseh E. Zerubbabel F. Uzziah

# Cross
Up from the grave

**Text:** Luke 22-24; Matthew 26-28;
Mark 14-16; John 18-21
**Memory verse:** 1 Corinthians 15:3–4

Can you think of a time when you did something wrong and then tried to hide or cover up what you did? Just as Adam and Eve tried to 'cover up' their shame by sewing fig leaves together, many people today try to 'cover up' their sin on their own. Some think that giving to the poor, attending church, being baptized or living a good life will allow them entrance into Heaven. But sin (disobedience to the commands of God), *any* sin, separates us from the Holy Creator God, and nothing that *we* manufacture will allow us to live forever with God.

Read through 'Cross' with your students, having them look up the Bible verses as you come to them.

(For a more detailed comparison between Adam and Jesus Christ, see 'First Adam–Last Adam,' <www.AnswersInGenesis.org/first_adam>.)

Ask your students, 'Do you know for certain that your name is written in the Lamb's Book of Life?' Explain it this way:

> Heaven is a free gift (Romans 6:23) offered by God to all who will receive it. We receive that free gift by repenting and having faith in Jesus Christ (i.e. who He is and what He did for us, Acts 20:21) for our salvation from sin (Romans 10:9; John 14:6; Acts 4:12).

Now read 'The old rugged cross' in this week's handout. As this article points out, the death and Resurrection of Jesus are not things that can be duplicated. They cannot be *proven* scientifically because they were one-time events. We know and understand what we do about Jesus Christ because of the words of Scripture. In the same way, the events of *Creation* were one-time events—they cannot be proven scientifically because they happened in the past. But God tells us in His Word that He created in six normal-length days, and He tells us that Jesus Christ (the God-man) died and rose again, so we can believe it because God never lies.

We discussed the *Catastrophe* of Noah's day a few weeks ago. Jesus referred to this event while He was on Earth.

### ◆ Read Matthew 24:37-39; Luke 17:27.

Some of His students also mention this event as true history in the books they wrote.

### ◆ Read Hebrews 11:7; 1 Peter 3:20; 2 Peter 2:5; 3:6.

Go over 'Noah's Ark and Jesus Christ' with your students, having them read the verses shown.

'Up from the grave He arose!' provides responses to some common claims by those who believe that, although Jesus may have been a real, historical person, He did not rise from the dead as the Bible claims. But we know the place where Jesus was buried is now empty—there is no body in it (John 19:39–20:8). The people who claim Jesus did not rise from the dead have made up stories about where the body went. This section refutes those claims and affirms the Biblical account that God raised Jesus from the dead.

## ◆ Discussion questions

1. Why did Jesus need to die on the Cross?

   To take away the sin introduced by Adam (by paying the penalty for it) and to conquer death (a result of that sin) so that we can have eternal life.

2. How do we know Christ rose from the dead?

   Ultimately, because of the words of Scripture—God tells us in His Word that He rose from the dead.

## ◆ Activity ideas

What was the culture like during Jesus' day? Who was in power at that time?

## ◆ If you have time ...

Finish with the 'Do you know your Bible?' and 'Let there be fun!' sections on the last page of the handout.

## ◆ Additional resource

'Q&A: Jesus Christ,' <www.AnswersInGenesis.org/JesusChrist>

'The Seven C's of History' (Creation, Corruption, Catastrophe, Confusion, Christ, Cross, Consummation) help us remember the big events which have affected—and will affect—the history of the universe.

'Christ Jesus ... who, being in the form of God ... was made in the likeness of men. And being found in fashion as a man, he humbled himself and became obedient unto death, even the death of the cross' (Philipians 2:5–8).

## The First Adam

Our first 'parent,' Adam, did not lead the perfect life he should have. He disobeyed his Creator's command not to eat from the Tree of the Knowledge of Good and Evil. Because of God's judgment on this one act of rebellion, the entire creation, which was originally perfect (Genesis 1:31), became subject to death and corruption. Because of Adam's sin, and because we sin personally, we all die (Romans 5:12–19).

## The Last Adam

Around 4,000 years after Adam disobeyed, God sent the perfect sacrifice, in the form of His Son, Jesus Christ, to take away the sin of the world, fulfilling the promise God made in Genesis 3:15. Jesus is called the 'Last Adam' in 1 Corinthians 15:45, and He came to restore the fellowship with the Creator that was broken by Adam's sin.

Adam disobeyed God's command not to eat the forbidden fruit; Jesus fulfilled the Creator's purpose that He die for the sin of the world.

The First Adam brought death into the world through his disobedience; the Last Adam (Jesus Christ) brought eternal life with God through His obedience (1 Corinthians 15:21–22).

Because God is perfectly holy, He must punish sin—either the sinner himself, or a substitute to bear His wrath.

God Himself made the first sacrifice for sin by killing an animal (this was the first death in God's creation) after Adam disobeyed (Genesis 3:21). But we should not offer animal sacrifices for sin any more. This is because the Lamb of God (John 1:29; Revelation 5:12) was sacrificed once for all (Hebrews 7:27). Jesus bore God's wrath on our sin by dying in our place (Isaiah 53:6). So all those who believe in Him will be saved from the ultimate penalty for sin (eternal separation from God), and will live with Him forever.

But Jesus Christ, the Creator of all things (John 1:1–3; Colossians 1:15–16), was not defeated by death. He rose three days after He

was crucified, showing that He has power over all things, including death, the 'last enemy' (1 Corinthians 15:26)!

This is why the Apostle Paul says, 'O death, where is your sting? O grave, where is your victory?... But thanks be to God who gives us the victory through our Lord Jesus Christ' (1 Corinthians 15:55, 57).

When we believe in the Lord Jesus Christ and understand what He has done for us, we are passed from death into life (John 5:24). The names of those who receive Him are written in the Lamb's Book of Life (Revelation 13:8; 17:8)—when they die, they will go to be with Him forever (John 3:16)!

# The old rugged Cross

**On a hill far away, stood an old rugged Cross, the emblem of suffering and shame ...**

About 2,000 years ago, some nations, such as the Romans, Persians or Phoenicians, executed many hundreds of criminals by nailing or strapping them to a rough, wooden pole or cross, and left them to die slowly and painfully. This was one of the worst causes of death possible, so it was normally used for the lowest of criminals, slaves and traitors. The victim was often flogged, stripped and made to carry a part of the cross to the place of execution, passing by crowds of people who mocked and teased him.

The earthly life of one person who suffered this death is recorded in four books written in the first century AD, and his life is mentioned in other historical accounts (such as the writings of Josephus and Cornelius Tacitus) as well. Guided by the Holy Spirit, four Jewish men (Matthew, a tax collector; John Mark, a student of the Apostle Peter; Luke, a doctor; and John, a fisherman) wrote about the life of the man known as Jesus the Messiah. The difference between Jesus and the hundreds of others who died on a cross is that He was completely God and completely man. He did not deserve to be crucified (He lived a perfect life) and He did not stay in the grave. Three days after He was buried, He rose from the dead—His *Resurrection*.

## He lives!

Paul (who saw the risen Christ) tells us that it is important that Jesus truly did rise again because '... if Christ is not raised, your faith is foolish ... . We are of all men most miserable' (1 Corinthians 15:14, 17). After Jesus rose from the dead, He met with His disciples (including the writers of the books of John and Matthew; and Peter, who informed Mark). He commanded them to tell people about the Creator who came to save the world from the curse of sin (Matthew 28:19–20; Revelation 4:11; 5:9). Then He went back to Heaven to prepare a place for those who believe in Him (John 13:2–3).

Just as 'science' cannot prove that Jesus rose from the dead, it also cannot prove that God created everything in six days. In fact, 'science' can't prove *any* event from history, because it is limited in dealings about the past. Historical events are known to be true because of *reliable eye-witness accounts*. Similarly, there are reliable eyewitness accounts that Jesus' tomb was empty after three days, and that He later appeared to as many as 500 people at once (1 Corinthians 15:6).

Most importantly, we know that both the Resurrection and Creation are true because God, the most reliable eyewitness of all, who never lies and knows everything, tells us in His Word that these things happened.

Dr Luke

# Noah's Ark and Jesus Christ

## Did you know that Noah's Ark and Jesus have some very important things in common?

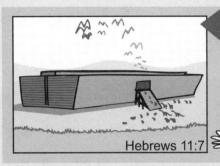

Hebrews 11:7

**Both are real & historical.**

Noah's Ark is not a fairy tale. It's part of history!

Jesus really came to Earth just as the Bible says.

1 John 4:14

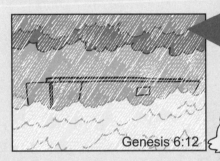

Genesis 6:12

**Both are God's provision to escape His judgments on man's sin.**

God told Noah to build the Ark to survive the Flood.

Jesus provides the way to escape God's final Judgment!

John 3:17    John 5:24

Genesis 7:23

**God's way of escape is the ONLY way!**

No matter what people outside the Ark tried to do to survive, it didn't work.

Outside of Jesus, you cannot get to Heaven.

There are many ways to Heaven!    There are many gods.    There is no God!    Jesus is not God.

John 14:6

Look at Noah's big boat!

HA

HA

What a silly thing to build!

Luke 17:27

**Many reject God's provided way of escape.**

The Flood killed all the people in the world except for the eight on the Ark.

Most people will not go to Heaven.

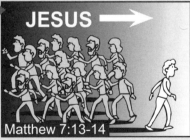

JESUS →

Matthew 7:13-14

Come into the Ark and be saved!

2 Peter 2:5

**Invitations given to escape God's judgment.**

It's too late for the people of Noah's day.

It's not too late for you to escape God's final Judgment!

**Romans 6:23**
For the wages of sin is death, but the gift of God is eternal life through Jesus Christ our Lord.

**John 3:16**
For God so loved the world that He gave His only-begotten Son, that whoever believes in Him should not perish but have everlasting life.

## DO YOU KNOW YOUR BIBLE?

In Genesis, God cursed the Earth with something His Son, Jesus, later wore on the Cross. What is it?

ANSWER: Thorns
The Curse: Genesis 3:17-18
The Crown: John 19:2-6

## LET THERE BE FUN!

See if you can find the 12 hidden words in the Cross word find. Look up, down, foreward and backward.

ADAM
DISOBEY

JESUS
CROSS
NAILS

SIN
FORGIVEN
DEAD
TOMB

RAISED
ALIVE
HEAVEN

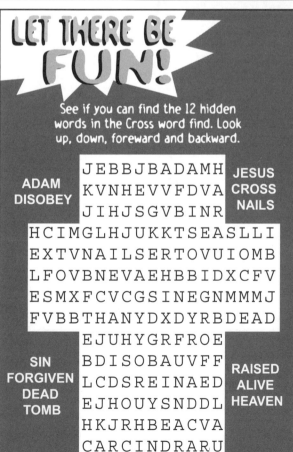

```
J E B B J B A D A M H
K V N H E V V F D V A
J I H J S G V B I N R
H C I M G L H J U K K T S E A S L L I
E X T V N A I L S E R T O V U I O M B
L F O V B N E V A E H B B I D X C F V
E S M X F C V C G S I N E G N M M M J
F V B B T H A N Y D X D Y R B D E A D
E J U H Y G R F R O E
B D I S O B A U V F F
L C D S R E I N A E D
E J H O U Y S N D D L
H K J R H B E A C V A
C A R C I N D R A R U
```

## Up from the grave He arose!

There are those who do not believe the historical accounts that Jesus really died and rose again. They have made up many stories to try to explain why the tomb where Jesus was buried is now empty.

- Some say Jesus just fainted while on the Cross, later revived in the cool tomb and then left. But ... Jesus would have had to unwrap Himself from the grave clothes, push aside the stone (which was too heavy to be moved by a single man) across the entrance to the tomb, and then walk past the soldiers outside. He would have been too weak to do this, and the guards would have stopped Him. Further, the Roman soldier pierced Him with a spear while He was still on the Cross, and the blood and water that flowed from this wound showed that He was truly dead.

- Others believe the disciples stole Jesus' body and then lied, saying He arose. But ... the disciples would not have made it past the tomb guards without the guards noticing them. Most of the disciples later died for their belief that Jesus arose—they would not have died for something they knew to be a lie.

- Some suggest the Romans or Jews removed Jesus' body from the tomb. But ... these two groups of people had no reason to do so—in fact, they would have wanted a body in the tomb to stop any stories that Jesus had risen. And when the followers of Christ began saying that they had seen Him alive, the Jews or Romans had only to produce the body showing the Christians' claims to be false—yet they didn't.

Still others say the story that Jesus rose from the dead is just a myth or legend. But ... the Gospels were written between 25 and 65 years after the crucifixion of Christ—far too little time for a myth to develop because eyewitnesses to the events were still around at that time to answer any questions. Further, many of those who saw Jesus after His Resurrection did not like Him. They would have certainly corrected the reports that claimed they had seen Him.

# $\mathcal{C}$onsummation
Back to 'very good'

**Text:** Revelation 21-22
**Memory verse:** Revelation 21:1

Introduction

We have talked, in the past, about the authors of the Gospels. One of those authors, Luke, was a doctor, someone who provides help to those who are sick. In the very beginning of creation, doctors would not have been necessary because there was no such thing as disease or sickness. Adam and Eve were completely healthy.

Make a list with your students of other jobs that people have today that wouldn't have been necessary if Adam hadn't sinned.

Because death and disease, thorns and thistles are only a temporary part of God's creation, they will one day be no more. The last 'C' of History—Consummation—will take place in the future.

Read 'Consummation!' and look up the Bible verses as you come to them.

*Consummation: fulfillment; the ultimate goal or end; completion

◆ **Read Romans 8:18-23; Acts 3:19-21; 2 Peter 3:10, 13; Revelation 21:1–22:6.**

These verses contain descriptions of the new heavens and new Earth and new Jerusalem. As you read the passages, have your students make a list of all the things that will be in the new heavens/Earth, where everything will once again be perfect, that *are not* in this present fallen world, and list all the things that will not be in the new heavens/Earth, that *are* in this present world.

Examples:

| New heavens and Earth | Present heavens and Earth |
|---|---|
| No tears | Tears |
| No pain/suffering | Pain/suffering |
| No death | Death |
| No need for sun/moon to provide light | Sun/moon provide light |
| Day only | Day and night |
| Light provided by God Himself | Light provided by sun, moon, stars |
| Water of life | No water of life |
| Tree of life | No tree of life |
| Saints | Sinners and saints |
| Righteousness will dwell there | Sin is rampant now |
| No more Curse of sin | Under the Curse of sin |
| Complete health | Disease, sickness |

Now read 'Promises and prophecies' and 'Back to "very good."' Point out to your students that because all have sinned, we all, in a sense, share in the corruption we experience today.

Read the 'Did you know ... ?' page.

## ◆ Discussion questions

1. Review.  List and describe each of the *7 C's of History.*

2. What things are your students dealing with now that they won't have to deal with in the new heavens and Earth (e.g. sickness, loss of loved ones)?

## ◆ Activity ideas

Research the various precious stones mentioned in Revelation 21:18-21.  What does each of the stones look like?  How much are they worth today?

'The Seven C's of History' (Creation, Corruption, Catastrophe, Confusion, Christ, Cross, Consummation) help us remember the big events which have affected—and will affect—the history of the universe.

'Then I saw a new heaven and a new earth; for the first heaven and the first earth passed away ...' (Revelation 21:1).

In the beginning, God created a perfect world. It was a beautiful place—full of life, without death, disease, pain or suffering. Adam's disobedience changed all that. When he ate the fruit God had told him not to eat, sin and death entered the world (Romans 5:12). This corruption changed the world so much that what we see today is only a reflection of the world that was. Adam's sin led to the catastrophe of Noah's day, the confusion at Babel and the death of Christ on the Cross.

## Is there an end in sight?

Death has been around almost as long as humans have. Sometimes it might seem as if it is a permanent part of God's creation. Romans 8 tells us the whole of creation is suffering because of Adam's sin. It might seem as if there is no end to the suffering brought about by this act of disobedience. Of course, none of us can say that we have not also disobeyed God in our own lives (Romans 3:23; 1 John 1:10), so all of us in a sense share in the blame for what we see around us.

However, God, in His great mercy, has promised to not leave His creation in its sinful state. He has promised to do away with the corruption Adam brought into the world. He offers us this salvation through His Son. Also, He has promised to remove, in the future, the Curse He placed on His creation (Revelation 22:3)!

He will make a new heaven and a new Earth one day—one which we can't even begin to imagine (2 Peter 3:13). In this new place there will be no death, no crying, no pain (Revelation 21:4). Nobody will be sad.

As those who have repented and believed in what Jesus did for us on the Cross, we can look forward to this new heaven and Earth, knowing we will enjoy God forever in a wonderful place. The corruption that was introduced in the Garden of Eden will be taken away by God, giving us, once again, a perfect place to live.

Noah and his 'Ark'? Ha! What's the Ark going to float on?!

HA HA HA HA

OH NO!

# Then ...

During the time of Noah, people laughed while Noah obediently built the boat God had commanded him to build. They mocked him as he told them God was going to judge their wickedness with a worldwide flood. They scorned Noah's preaching about their need to repent and turn to their Creator before it was too late. They rejected the Lord God who had created their ancestor Adam. All those who did not believe what Noah said and who did not follow him onto the Ark died in the Flood that God sent as punishment for the people's disobedience (sin).

# Now ...

Today, many people deny that the global Flood in Noah's day ever occurred. They refuse to listen to those who obediently preach about the Creator who came to Earth to redeem His creation from the curse of sin. They mock the very words of God that say He created all things in six days. They have rejected the Lord God who created their ancestor Adam and are disobedient to His commands. They scorn the warning that God will once again judge His creation for the wickedness of men.

Jesus' student, Peter, wrote his second letter to the Jewish believers scattered throughout Asia around AD 66. In it, he discusses the people mentioned above, saying, 'There shall come in the last days scoffers, walking after their own lusts and saying, "Where is the promise of His coming? For since the fathers fell asleep, all things continue as they were from the beginning of the creation." For of this they are willfully ignorant: that by the Word of God the heavens were of old, and the earth standing out of the water and in the water, whereby the world as it then was, being overflowed with water, perished' (2 Peter 3:3-6).

Just as the unbelievers in Noah's day were punished for their wickedness, so the unbelievers today will be punished for their sin (2 Peter 3:7). And just as God has kept His promise never again to flood the entire Earth (our reminder of this promise is the rainbow), so He will keep His promise to one day create a new heavens and Earth for those who believe in Him (Isaiah 65:17; 2 Peter 3:10, 13).

The Bible isn't true! 'Science' has shown that! God didn't judge the Earth with water, and He's not going to judge with fire!

The Bible tells us God originally created the world 'very good.' It was perfect!

But Romans 8:22 says, 'for we know that the whole creation groans and travails in pain together until now.'

Something has changed this world. Now we see bad and good. The 'good' things are just remnants of that original 'very good' Creation, while the bad things were a later intrusion, not part of what God originally created.

In today's world we have...

**Beauty & Ugliness** · **Pleasure & Pain** · **Health & Sickness** · **Happiness & Sorrow** · **Life & Death**

Some people blame God for the bad THINGS in our world.

God, why did you do this?

But it's not God's fault!

The bad we see in this world is man's fault. Man's sin brought the curse of death and corrupted the whole creation.

However, God knew all this would happen, and He had a plan to rescue his children from this cursed world.

We think of this present world as home, but it is only temporary. God has new heavens and a new Earth in store for those who believe in His Son's death and Resurrection.

Those who don't believe in Jesus' death and Resurrection will have a different eternal home.
2 Thessalonians 1:8-10
Revelation 20:12-15

Once again, God's children will enjoy a perfect creation. This new home will last forever. All the bad things will be no more. How great it will be when God restores His Creation, back to 'VERY GOOD'!

Make sure this new world will be your future home, too! John 3:16; Romans 10:8-10

# Did you know...

**But, beloved, be not ignorant of this one thing: that with the Lord one day is as a thousand years, and a thousand years as one day (2 Peter 3:8).**

Some people use the above verse to claim that each of the 'days' mentioned in Genesis 1 could have been a thousand years long, rather than normal length.

However, the verse says one day is **as** (i.e. *like*) a thousand years. This is a figure of speech called a *simile*, and it teaches that God is outside of time because He is the Creator of time. It is not defining day, because it doesn't say 'a day **is** a thousand years.' In fact, the figure of speech is so effective here precisely because the word 'day' is *literal* and contrasts so vividly with (a literal) 1,000 years. In fact, Peter is referring to Psalm 90:4, which also says that 1,000 years is 'like a watch in the night.' So if these people were right, they would also have to say that a night watch could last 1,000 years!

It is always important to read Scripture passages 'in context.' This means paying special attention to the verses surrounding the passage you are studying. In context, Peter is saying, in 2 Peter 3:8, that although it may seem a long time to us until the Lord keeps His promise and comes again, it is not very long at all to the Lord.

*Grandpa, when is Jesus coming back? I've been waiting for Him my whole life!*

*That's a long time to wait ... to us!*

---

## DO YOU KNOW YOUR BIBLE?

Heaven will not have two specific things that God created in His original creation on Day 4. Do you know what they are?

ANSWER : A sun and a moon. The glory of God will illuminate Heaven (Revelation 21:23)!

---

## LET THERE BE FUN!

### Eden or Heaven or BOTH?

See if you can tell if the following things are from the Garden of Eden, or Heaven, or both.

1 No death

2 Streets of gold

3 Tree of Life

4 Precious stones

5 Fruit tree

6 Day and night

7 Perfect relationship with God

ANSWERS: 1. Both 2. Heaven 3. Both 4. Both 5. Both 6. Eden 7. Both